WAYS
TO KEEP
YOUR
LOVER

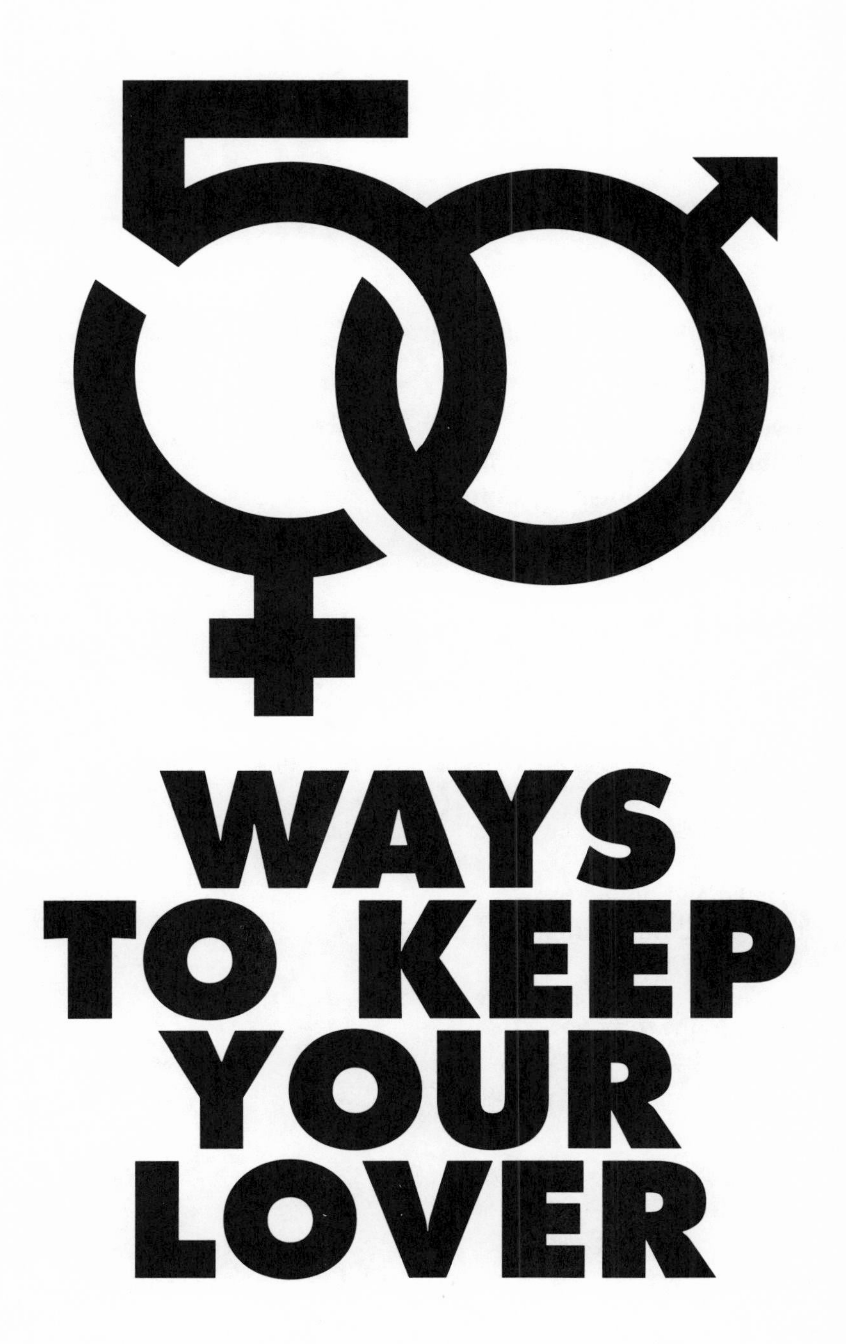

WAYS TO KEEP YOUR LOVER

by John Ingram Walker, M.D.

Lynn Grove Press
Published under the imprint:
Lifeworks Publishing Company
P.O. Box 353
Red River, New Mexico 87558

Manuscript Preparation by Nanette Burkhardt.

Copy Editing by Lynette Weaver.

Typesetting by David Nielsen, Historical Publications.

Cover Design by Lee Rader, Lee Rader Designs.

Printed and bound in
the United States of America
by BookCrafters.

ISBN 0-9621073-3-6

Preface

Strange how the unconscious works for us, slowly simmering ideas outside of our awareness until they emerge from our minds fully cooked, ready to be enjoyed. On December 19, 1991, I awoke from a sound sleep with the idea for this book fully prepared. My first thought upon awakening was— *50 Ways To Keep Your Lover*—what a wonderful idea for a book! I went to my office and within three hours had dictated what would prove to be the main ideas in this recipe for lasting relationships. All that remained was the rewriting, to trim off all the unnecessary fat, if you will, so that you could have a book that had only the necessary ingredients, simply told, that would enable you to have a lasting, loving relationship.

Now from where did this idea, this recipe come? Upon minimal reflection that answer is an easy one. My daughter, Wende, was soon to be married. Evidently as father of the bride, I had been thinking of this grand occasion more than I realized and my unconscious had produced a book that would be useful to Wende and her husband-to-be, Greg, and would also benefit anyone who would like to keep a meaningful relationship.

For whom is this book written then? Well—Wende and Greg and all newly-weds, of course. There is much basic information that can help them get started on building a lasting relationship. Anyone who looks at the text carefully will see that the book would hold special interests for those who have been married for five, ten or fifteen years—the period when marriages are most threatened by the predilection to drift or to stagnate. And the book is even useful for "the old pros"—those who have been married for 25 years or more. Indeed, Vicki and I, with 26 years of marital struggles and blessings, have found the words that my unconscious has written helpful reminders. So now the answer to the question has come full circle: this book is for anyone who wants to keep a lover.

A word of warning: you'll find no poetry in this prose and very little humor—only rules, regulations, suggestions and reminders, basic food for thoughtful lovers, food that will nurture a marriage. I hope you will read and reread this book and benefit for a lifetime from the sustenance found here.

John Ingram Walker, M.D.
December, 1991

Acknowledgements

Of all the material I have read, heard, or viewed on loving relationships two items stand out—the book, *The Road Less Traveled*, by M. Scott Peck, M.D. and the videotape *Hidden Keys To Loving Relationships*, by Gary Smalley. I recommend these materials to anyone wanting to build lasting relationships. I am grateful for the help Chris Weichsel gave on Rule #35. I thank my patients who through the years have taught me more about human behavior than all the books in my library. My daughter, Wende, and my son, Brad, have contributed much more to my emotional and spiritual growth than I have to theirs. (Children teach life lessons, if we are quiet and listen.) My wife Vicki has been most essential to my life's joy and development. Through the years she has supported, encouraged, tolerated and sustained me. She has cried and laughed with me. She has suffered and enjoyed with me. But most important she has loved me. Who could ask for more!

Dedication

To my daughter, Wende, and her fiancé, Greg. May their love last forever.

Also this book is for Brad and his SMU roommate, Keny, who, when they find the right woman to love, will need all the help they can get.

50 Ways To Keep Your Lover

1 Offer Security
2 Talk To Your Lover
3 Romance Your Lover
4 Hug And Caress Your Lover
5 Praise Your Lover
6 Provide Sexual Intimacy
7 Act Your Love
8 Show Care And Concern
9 Be There
10 Be Faithful
11 Show Enthusiasm
12 Honor Your Lover
13 Date Your Lover

32 Say No
33 Listen
34 Be A Good Parent
35 Have A Strong Financial Base
36 Believe In A Higher Power
37 Relax
38 Use I-Messages
39 Think Positively
40 Love Yourself
41 Pay Attention To Daily Disciplines
42 Live Each Day Fully
43 Control Anger
44 Forget The Past
45 Enjoy The Ordinary
46 Accept Change
47 Give Compliments
48 Stay In Shape
49 Do Your Best
50 Adopt A Holistic Life-Style

Love is patient, love is kind. It does not envy, it does not boast, it is not proud. It is not rude, it is not self-seeking, it is not easily angered, it keeps no record of wrongs.

Love does not delight in evil but rejoices with the truth. It always protects, always trusts, always hopes, always perseveres.

I Corinthians 13:4-7

1

Offer Security

To Keep Your Lover, Offer Security. This one's for men. Men, if you want to keep your woman, exhibit emotional stability and security. Women want strong, confident, self-assured men who will supply them the essential material comforts, emotional stability and permanence. Women want to know that they will be cared for and that they have a man who is dependable, consistent, steady and reassuring.

Women like men who, to use Hemingway's term, exhibit grace under pressure. In contrast to bravado or dominance, grace under pressure reflects quiet confidence and self-assurance—an inner power devoid of the desire to control. Paradoxically because there is no desire to dominate, men with self-assurance have a magnetic quality that pull women to them. Self-assurance is the most important trait a man can pass along to his children and is the basic quality that women seek in men.

Tell her every day you love her, men, but don't grovel. If you keep talking about how much you miss her, or that you are afraid she will leave you, then she may think you are weak and become disenchanted. Just be steady. Steadiness offers security.

2

Talk To Your Lover

To Keep Your Lover, Talk More. Men, this one's aimed at you too. Women like to talk (I bet you don't need a psychiatrist to tell you that one) and to be talked to. They want to hear what you are doing and what you are thinking. It's important for lovers to set aside some time for daily uninterrupted conversation.

Ann Moir in *Brain Sex: The Real Difference Between Men and Women* contends that the brain of a women processes information differently resulting in different priorities. In general, women are more right-brained. They're into feelings. They are nurturers. Now before you start calling me chauvinistic, let me hasten to say that we are talking about averages here. For example, most men will be taller than most women, but any woman may be taller than any man.

Because of brain differences **most** women (notice I wrote most) talk more than **most** men. Studies have shown that the average man talks about 12,000 words a day; the average woman talks about 25,000 words a day. When a man comes home from work he has used up his 12,000 words and a women is only half-way there. So men, you need to find a time to talk with your woman. Perhaps early in the morning before you have used up your 12,000 words for the day would be best.

Talk about anything, women especially like to hear about your successes and your feelings. Remember, feelings turn women on. So to keep the conversation flowing you might ask her, "How does that make you feel?"

3

Romance Your Lover

To Keep Your Lover, Be Romantic. Men, this one's especially meant for you also. Again, studies by Dr. Moir and others indicate that women may be more romantic because of brain connections. Researchers have discovered the corpus callosum—the fibers that connect the right and left hemispheres of the brain—are more prominent in women than men, giving them more artistic and verbal skills while men have more white matter in the brain—material that facilitates sensory and motor coordination. Thus, men sail boats while women write poems about sailing.

So, men, the next time you go sailing with your love hold her and whisper in her ear. Let someone else sail the boat. Remember men: "sweet nothings" in time are more valuable than $1000 gifts too late. They're also cheaper.

Women like to be romanced. They enjoy a walk on the beach holding hands. They like sitting out on the patio when the moon is full. They like to have their birthdays, anniversaries and Valentine's Day remembered. They like candy and flowers sent spontaneously.

Hint: Don't send them flowers when you've messed up. They can see through that one a mile away and are likely to hit you over the head with the flower pot when you come home. Instead send them flowers on a routine day and attach a note, something like this: "For an extraordinary woman on an ordinary day."

4

Hug And Caress Your Lover

To Keep Your Lover, Hug And Caress More. Again, men, this one's especially for you. After security, conversation and romance, then women want physical contact. Women like to be hugged. They like to hold hands. They like to have their backs rubbed and they like to be caressed. The path to sexual intimacy begins with understanding what women want before sex.

According to Helen Singer Kaplan, M.D., Ph.D. in *The New Sex Therapy,* there appear to be some gender differences between male and female sexual arousal. Hugs, caresses, gentle kissing "seem to be relatively more potent erotic stimuli for women in our culture than are visual ones." In contrast visual stimuli are generally more exciting for men. Not only do women need more hugs and shows of affection on a day to day basis, they also need more caressing, more foreplay to fully enjoy the sexual act.

Unfortunately some men have a difficult time demonstrating physical affection. Men, if you have this problem, work on improving your ability to feel comfortable with the physical demonstrations of affection. Just practice hugging or kissing her every day. And it's all right just to hold your lover without leading to anything else. Hold her, men, and you'll keep her.

5

Praise Your Lover

To Keep Your Lover, Use Praise. Women, this one's especially for you. Men want their women to tell them what a good job they've done, what fantastic athletes or hunters they are, what achievers they are. So, women, if you want to improve your relationship, begin by offering up some honest praise.

Remember, women, most men are left-brained. (Understand that I'm writing about generalities here, but generalities, please excuse the expression, are, generally true). Men like facts. Men are basically doers, achievers. They are task oriented. They like to get the job done. Think of men as hunters. They like to conquer.

Put a man in an automobile and he will attempt to conquer the highway: drive non-stop 483 miles to Dumas, Texas, with no restroom breaks, running out of gas as he tops the last rise. Men are taught to conquer pain: "Get up, boy, and shake it off. There's no bone showing." Men set out to conquer the golf course: "Let us hit through, ladies. We want to get in 36 holes today." Men hope to conquer the business world: "Making money is a way of keeping score."

So, women, men are simple: tell them that you appreciate them. The most important words most men can hear are these: "I'm proud of you." Use those words, women, and you will keep your man forever.

6

Provide Sexual Intimacy

To Keep Your Lover, Provide Sexual Intimacy. Men and women both enjoy sex, of course. But men perform much better if they get a lot of praise before the sexual act. Women do better if they are provided with security, meaningful conversation, romance, hugs and caresses prior to the sexual act.

Likewise, men, you need to remember that it takes longer for a woman to "warm up" during the sexual act. So men, you need to take more time. And women, you need to tell your man what you like and what excites you. Speak up. He can't read your mind and he is likely to think that if he's aroused you are aroused. The key to sexual intimacy is open communication. When you talk with each other, sex is more fun and more stimulating.

7

Act Your Love

To Keep Your Lover, Act Your Love. Lovers realize that love is more an act of will than it is a feeling. Romantic feelings pass, but the action of love persists forever. Genuine love is an extension of the self. When we love we focus on helping those we love grow emotionally, intellectually and spiritually. We can forget our own egos by creating happiness for our loved ones. Paradoxically the more we give of ourselves, the more we *extend* ourselves—the more we receive, the more we are replenished.

Psychoanalyst Alfred Adler, in his book, *What Life Should Mean To You*, says, ''It is the individual who is not interested in his fellow man who has the greatest difficulties in life and provides the greatest injury to others. It is from among such individuals that all human failures spring.'' Benjamin Franklin said, ''When you are good to others you are best to yourself.''

You act your love by living your life so others will be happy to see you. You act your love when you become less concerned about your individual desires and more interested in helping others become all they can be. You act your love by spreading joy and good will to everyone wherever you go.

And—you act your love by taking out the trash when no one asks you—or setting the table without being urged—or washing the dishes when you aren't importuned.

8

Show Care And Concern

To Keep Your Lover, Show Care And Concern. A good relationship requires care and concern. That means paying attention to voice inflection, body language, how words are expressed and what is *not* said. What is she worried about? What is troubling him? What makes her happy? What gives him peace of mind? Care and concern mean being sensitive to each other's needs.

The importance of care and concern is indicated in the wedding vow: "To have and to hold, from this day forward, for better, for worse, for richer, for poorer, in sickness and in health, to love and to cherish until death us do part, according to God's holy ordinance, and thereto I pledge thee my faith."

Joseph Campbell, the world's foremost authority on mythology writes, "In the middle ages a favorite image that occurs in many, many contexts is the wheel of fortune. There is the hub of the wheel, and there is the revolving rim of the wheel. For example, if you are attached to the rim of the wheel of fortune, you will be either above, going down, or at the bottom, coming up. But if you are at the hub, you are in the same place all of the time. That is the sense of the marriage vow—I take you in health or sickness, in wealth or poverty: going up or going down. But I take you as my center, and you are my bliss, not the wealth that you might bring me, not the social prestige, but you." With care and concern for your lover you stay centered on his/her needs and feelings.

9

Be There

To Keep Your Lover, Be There. A good marriage requires attention, being fully alive in the present.Perhaps a personal experience will best illustrate this point:

Several years ago my wife, Vicki, cheerfully entered my study where I was reading and relaxing. "John," she said, "guess who I saw at the office today—Ted Koeppel, the ABC news 'Nightline' man." Engrossed in my copy of *Sports Illustrated* I replied, "Um, that's interesting." A few seconds later I looked up and there was Vicki with a stunned expression on her face. She said, "You get after me for not spending time with you. Maybe I don't spend time with you because you're always in another zone." I realized that I had missed a wonderful opportunity to have a warm interchange of ideas with Vicki, an opportunity now lost and gone forever. Sadly I remembered an admonishment I had heard from speaker Jim Rohn, "Wherever you are, be there."

That day I pledged to Vicki that I would change, that I would work on "being there." That interchange has caused me to focus more and has improved our marriage considerably.

The experience made me keenly aware of Emerson's words, "The only gift is a portion of thyself." Lovers know that they can give more of themselves if they follow that simple rule, "Wherever you are, be there."

10

Be Faithful

To Keep Your Lover, Be Faithful. A good relationship requires faith in the other person, being certain of the other's reliability and commitment. Being faithful means being true. And trusting. Being faithful means avoiding jealousy. Jealousy only eats away at our love. Being faithful means that we keep our commitments to ourselves and our loved ones. Faith requires that we communicate to each other what we expect and want in the relationship. Faith insists on being true, despite disappointment, pain, frustration and misunderstandings. Faith mandates a commitment to a state of continuing concern for the loved one.

11

Show Enthusiasm

To Keep Your Lover, Show Enthusiasm. To be truly loving requires enthusiasm. We can't be bored and boring and be loving. We can't be frantically running from event to event and be loving. Being enthusiastic means thinking, feeling, laughing, being receptive and engaged in whatever is going on.

If you lack enthusiasm, do as William James suggests. William James, the American father of psychological pragmatism, postulated the "as if" principle. James taught that you could cultivate a desired attitude by acting "as if" you had it. To become enthusiastic, act enthusiastic. Practice being enthusiastic about everyday things: sunrises, sunsets, fleecy clouds against a blue sky, a gentle rain, soft falling snow. Talk enthusiastically to your loved one, "The steaks were great! You are the gourmet griller of Greenville. I'm proud of you." Tell yourself you enjoy your work. Tell yourself you find people fascinating. Expand your vocabulary. Use enthusiastic words: terrific, fantastic, tremendous, magnificent, outstanding.

German philosopher Nietzsche said, "Nothing ever succeeds which exuberant spirits have not helped to produce." Enthusiasm will help your love succeed. Enthusiasm brings a level of vitality and awareness to romance. Enthusiasm is the ultimate replenishing gift, the radiant blessing of love.

12

Honor The Loved One

To Keep Your Lover, Honor The Loved One. The essence of love is honor: the conviction that each is the most important person in the other's life. This means we have to show that conviction daily in our words and actions. We must value our loved ones and treat our loved ones accordingly. Honor, then, gives a new dimension to intimacy. With honor there's a coming together of two who share strengths, weaknesses, thoughts, feelings, laughter and the joyful, regenerative magic of touch.

Gary Smalley in his videotape, *Hidden Keys To Loving Relationships*, insists that genuine love is based on honor for the loved one. Gary makes this point clear in his seminars by passing around a genuine Stradivarius violin. The audience touches it with great care and respect, amidst "oh's" and "ah's." They know the violin's value and treat it accordingly. In the same manner we must honor our loved ones. We must treat our loved ones as the most valuable object in our lives.

13

Date Your Lover

To Keep Your Lover, Go Out With Your Lover One Night A Week Alone. Being alone together adds romance to the relationship. To be alone together does not require a lot of money. You can go to the dollar movie; you can go to the Dairy Queen; you can go for a walk in the park; but just go out together alone, you and your lover and talk with each other and get to know each other intimately. Remember: one night a week—will keep the love you seek.

14

Get Away With Your Lover

To Keep Your Lover, Get Away With Your Lover. A weekend break once a month—just the two of you together—adds spice to the relationship and gives you and your lover something to look forward to. Again you don't have to spend a lot of money and you don't have to go far away. Just get away. You can leave about noon on Saturday and return in the afternoon on Sunday. You can get Grandma or the neighbors or a baby-sitter to watch the kids. I tell people who live where I live, the most beautiful little city in Texas, New Braunfels, to go to San Antonio, 25 miles down the road, to have a great time. I tell people whom I see in San Antonio that they can go to New Braunfels and have a terrific time. I tell the people who live in Poteet, Texas, they can go anywhere and have a good time. The point is get away with your lover and add romance to the relationship.

15

Ignore The Small Things

To Keep Your Lover, Ignore The Small Things. Sometimes little things, uncapped toothpaste tubes, dirty clothing piled on the floor, a messy room, can become intensely irritating and can be blamed for breaking up a marriage. Try to understand why small things loom large. Look for the problems behind the problem. If little things are eating away at you talk about the difficulties and try to put the issue in perspective. Instead of focusing on the small irritating things, focus on issues that really matter.

16

Don't Bring Up Old Problems

To Keep Your Lover, Don't Bring Up Old Problems. Following a disagreement, don't bring it up again. Understand that all relationships will be plagued by some disagreements, but when an argument is over, it's over. Let your lover know that you are hurt, but then forgive and forget. Don't keep punishing your lover by bringing up old problems.

17

Avoid Self Sacrifice

To Keep Your Lover, Avoid Self Sacrifice. Injudicious giving and destructive nurturing harm a relationship. "Giving" and "sacrifice" aren't love when the gift or the sacrifice interferes with the growth of your lover. For example, picking up after your loved one who has a total disregard for housecleaning is not an act of love. It is self-sacrifice. Love is extending yourself for the loved one's growth. When you "give yourself" by cleaning up after your lover makes a mess, you aren't helping your lover grow. You're not teaching your lover the value of self-discipline. Instead you are infantilising your lover. A loving act, in this case, would involve telling your lover that you are no longer cleaning up after him/her and that you want him/her to take care of his/her own messes. As M. Scott Peck, M.D. indicates, "Love must be manifested in confrontation as much as in beatific acceptance."

Those who genuinely love do so because they want to love. There is pleasure in extending the self for another's growth. There is **no** real pleasure in self-sacrifice. If you are extending yourself for the other's growth, you are loving. If you sacrifice yourself, you are not.

18

Be Independent

To Keep Your Lover, [illegible]
times you must be willir[illegible]
keep your lover. The g[illegible]
logically independent. [illegible]
the expectations of the [illegible]
don't marry because [illegible]
son. They marry becau[illegible]
committing themselves to the grow[illegible]
one.

The more you cling to another person, the more likely you are to drive that person away because clinging-dependency prevents growth in you and your lover. When you are smothering another person, you are retarding that person's growth.

The genuine lover is independent and sees the beloved as someone who has a separate identity. Likewise, the genuine lover has the courage to accept aloneness and separateness. Indeed there can be no true love without independence and separateness whereby the lovers help each other to continually take risks and grow.

To paraphrase Kahlil Gibran, lovers allow spaces in their togetherness and although they love one another they are not bound by love; instead of drinking from the same cup, they fill each other's cup; instead of eating from the same loaf, they give one another their bread; and though they quiver with the same music, they are as separate strings of a lute. As the pillars of a temple stand apart, lovers stand apart supporting each other.

19

Fight Fair

To Keep Your Lover, Fight Fair. Although most arguments are spur of the moment encounters, appropriate timing should be tried. Set aside some time for a constructive discussion. The environment for the discussion should be comfortable to both parties, offering privacy without restrictions, allowing the participants freedom to be open.

Participants in a fair fight must try at all times to keep eye contact with each other. Each participant should agree not to interrupt the other while the fight is going on. Each person is allowed a time to speak; then the other may talk.

Feedback for each participant is important. Each should share with the other what they have heard the other say so there will be no discrepancies.

Assumptions should not be made about anything. If one participant is unsure what the other is talking about, he/she should ask the other to be specific.

Each participant should attempt to convey to the other his or her feelings concerning the issues. This should be done by using "I" statements, such as "I feel . . . because . . . "

20

Remember: You Can't Change Your Lover

To Keep Your Lover, Remember: You Can't Change Your Lover. You cannot force another person to change. Read this again: You cannot force another person to change. Nagging won't work. Don't nag. If you must, bite your tongue until it bleeds to prevent nagging. Threats aren't helpful unless you follow through with what you threaten. Arguing will not change another person. Preaching won't work. Scolding always fails. Quarreling won't help. Coaxing is useless.

You can shape behavior and modify behavior, however. The way to shape behavior is to ask directly for what you want and then thank or praise your lover when it is given to you. If your lover's irresponsible behavior is leading to self-destruction, communicate verbally that you care enough to help him/her modify the behavior. If your lover is willing to make some modifications, ask what you can do to help. Both of you should then agree on a plan of action. A handshake, a hug, or a written agreement will help seal the contract. Then give praise for the improved behavior.

21

Ignore Bad Behavior

To Keep Your Lover, Ignore Bad Behavior. Don't nag. Don't hassle. Don't carp. If at all possible completely ignore bad behavior. The more you pay attention to bad behavior, the more the behavior pattern increases. The more you are able to ignore the bad behavior, the more likely it will go away.

There are two times when inappropriate behavior must be confronted:

▪ When the behavior is harmful to your loved one.

▪ When behavior is harmful to your relationship.

When inappropriate behavior must be confronted, simply say:

▪ "I feel your behavior (describe the behavior) is harming you. I would like for you to stop."

▪ "I feel your behavior (describe the behavior) is harming our relationship. I would like for you to stop."

22

Be Spontaneous

To Keep Your Lover, Be Spontaneous. Cultivate spontaneity by allowing your positive emotions to flow freely. Spontaneous activity involves helping others have fun while they help you have fun. Emotion, not effort, enhances play. Here are some tips on building spontaneity into your lifestyle:

- Quit work early or take time off when fatigue builds.
- Schedule vacations and keep them.
- Sustained effort toward a goal runs you down if not balanced by freedom, spontaneous feelings and laughter.
- Leisure should be a valuable force for good, not a drain on your emotions.
- You should laugh more than frown when playing golf, tennis, bridge, trivial pursuit, pictionary, etc. If not, change games.
- Try something new to stimulate creativity. Learn to play a musical instrument, paint, attend a drama class.
- Cultivate a hobby.

23

Give Feedback

To Keep Your Lover, Give Feedback. Remember that feedback is the hors d'oeuvre of championship lovers. Let your lover know directly what you like and what you don't like. Feedback is essential for a good relationship and is closely akin to asking for what you want. Remember you are not going to get what you want if you don't let the person know your desires and he/she won't know what you like if you are silent. Even excellent lovers are generally poor mind readers. Clairvoyance is for carnival side shows, not lovers.

Clarification: Feedback is *not* nagging. Feedback is a direct statement about what you see, think, feel, like, want, prefer.

24

Be Funny

To Keep Your Lover, Be Funny. Almost all surveys show that women desire a sense of humor in their men even more highly than they value good looks. Indeed a sense of humor is extremely attractive to a woman. Men like humorous women, too.

Now there are three levels of humor. One detracts from a good relationship; the other two enhance romance. Sarcasm, ridicule, and destructive humor should be avoided at all times. If you say "I'd rather bring my wife to the convention than kiss her good-bye," you'll flunk Romance 101. If your wife says, "I've had 12 happy years of married life, which is not bad for 18 years of marriage," she'll never book passage on the Love Boat.

On the other hand, belly-laugh humor—humor that provides a good laugh without being negative—can reduce anger, frustration, fear and stress. Belly-laugh humor requires that we see the incongruity of things.

The third type of humor—the highest form of humor—is cosmic humor which allows an appreciation of the paradoxes and absurdities of life. With the use of cosmic humor we refuse to take ourselves and our problems too seriously.

Clarification: If there is hostility in the humor, it's negative and should be avoided; if there's love and warmth in the humor, it's either belly-laugh or cosmic humor, and, thus, beneficial.

25

Be Fun-Loving

To Keep Your Lover, Be Fun-Loving. To keep your lover decide to be hopeful and fun-loving. Have a "bluebird on the shoulder" attitude that reflects a childlike joy for living. Here are some fun-loving tips:

- Surround yourself with people who fill you with joy and laughter.
- Be an inverse paranoid—think the world is out to do you good.
- Put on your "candid camera" glasses. When things get tough, try distancing yourself from your environment.
- Read or listen to humor regularly.
- Keep a humor collection—"Far Side" cartoons, Erma Bombeck columns, limericks, *Madd Magazines*, whatever tickles you.
- Remember that few things are absolute or sacred.
- Don't take yourself so seriously. Learn to laugh at your frailties and your mistakes. Humble self-acceptance of your imperfections is the highest form of humor.

26

Follow Your Bliss

To Keep Your Lover, Follow Your Bliss. To keep your lover find a way to follow your bliss, to do what you enjoy in a way that contributes to his/her growth. When we follow our bliss we give ourselves to something bigger than ourselves; we become involved totally in life; we work for the pleasure of working; we become committed to projects and people; our egos become secondary to our involvement.

To follow your bliss determine what you enjoy doing and start doing that more often. Spend your time in ways that bring fulfillment. Let the life you live reflect your values. Live your life as if you had only six months to live. Begin attempting those things that you were afraid to attempt in the past.

27

Live Your Epitaph

To Keep Your Lover, Live Your Epitaph. What would you like to see written on your own tombstone? Write your own epitaph. This way you'll start visualizing the person you want to be.

We've all heard the joke about the hypochondriac. He had written on his tombstone, "I told you I was sick." You can have your own epitaph come true also. Just write one out.

An excellent way to become a superb lover is to imagine that you have already died and then been allowed to return to life. This vision helps in two ways: 1) you focus on what's truly important in life—love, family, daily enjoyment of simple pleasures; and 2) you begin to lead your life in a way that you would like to be described. How would you like your lover to describe you—hard boiled, self centered, driven, intense—or romantic, thoughtful, kind, gentle, humorous, warm? Live the way you would like to be described.

28

Receive Love Gratefully

To Keep Your Lover, Receive Love Gratefully. Be open and receptive to the warmth of your loved one. Take compliments with deep felt appreciation and warm thanks. Realize that you are worthy of being loved. Cultivate a sense of worth. To put the issue poetically as Lerner and Lowe did in *Camelot*, lovers realize that they are, "A tiny drop in the great blue ocean of the sunlit sea but some of the drops do sparkle—some of the drops *do* sparkle."

29

Respect Yourself

To Keep Your Lover, Respect Yourself. Life offers unlimited opportunities for your emotional, intellectual, and spiritual growth. Respecting yourself means taking advantage of these opportunities. Growth is difficult. There exists a natural inclination to keep to the safe and easy way. Laziness often prevails. But real lovers, committed lovers, choose to transcend the easy path. This effort to transcend comes from love. When we love, we get off our duffs and get going. We elevate ourselves; we push ourselves; we become all we can be because we love enough to respect ourselves.

When we respect ourselves we realize that each of us has unique talents and abilities. Each of us has a holiness. Each of us can be a vibrant center of light and spirituality. Developing this vibrant center involves respect both for your lover and yourself. Respect compels us to grow and in growing we become more loving.

30

Endure Hardships

To Keep Your Lover, Endure Hardships. Lovers realize that all experiences, especially painful ones, offer an opportunity to learn and to grow.

Some of us go to extraordinary extremes to avoid hardship, to avoid our problems. Some of us had rather let our lovers leave than work on the problems that cause the split. When this happens, of course, our problems remain and we make the same mistakes with the next lover and the next.

A loving relationship requires the courage to face our problems and learn and change and grow from our hardships. M. Scott Peck, M.D. in his book, *The Road Less Traveled*, suggests there are four ways to endure hardships constructively: delay gratification, accept responsibility, commit to the truth, and cultivate flexibility. **Delaying gratification** simply means taking time to solve problems. **Accepting responsibility** requires continual self-examination so that we can realistically assess our duties to ourselves and our world. **Commitment to the truth** means that we strive to lead a life of total honesty to ourselves and others. **Flexibility** requires the capacity to assume responsibility for our behavior while letting go of those issues over which we have no control, striking a balance between conflicting goals, duties, and responsibilities. When we endure hardships, we experience the joy that understanding, acceptance and commitment bring.

31

Plan A Fulfilled Life

To Keep Your Lover, Plan A Fulfilled Life. Socrates said, "The unexamined life is not worth living." Aristotle expanded Socrates' statement when he said, "The unplanned life is not worth examining." So lovers plan their lives. They write down their personal goals, their career goals, their self-improvement goals, and go after them with vigor, enthusiasm and joy. They read their goals daily and ask the question, "Am I doing those things that will enable me to reach my goals?" They love better because they live life better.

A planned life is a fulfilled life—fulfillment in personal, family, career and spiritual paths. Fulfillment is the ability to love, enjoy work and have fun. Fulfillment is making a difference—a positive difference. Fulfillment is making the world a little bit better because you existed. To be fulfilled requires a planned life. Are you doing those things that will lead to a life of fulfillment?

32

Say No

To Keep Your Lover, Say "No" To Unimportant Projects. If you don't control your time someone else will and you will be so worn-out that you can't love.

How many projects are you committed to right now that you really don't enjoy? More than likely you said "yes" to these projects because you didn't want to disappoint someone, indirectly indicating that you valued that other person more than you value yourself. To value yourself more appropriately, you must learn to say "no." Saying "no" immediately saves everyone a great deal of frustration and allows you enough energy to love.

To help determine your desire to be involved in a project ask yourself these questions:

- Will I enjoy this project?
- Do I have time for this project?
- Will the benefits of this project outweigh the difficulties?
- Are the obligations to this project more important than other aspects of my life?

If you can answer "yes" to all four of these questions then the project is probably worthy of your time. If not, say "no," leaving time for your lover.

33

Listen

To Keep Your Lover, Listen. Listening requires that you put aside everything else—lay down the newspaper, turn off the TV, stop knitting, block out your own worries and preoccupations and focus completely on your loved one. True listening means that you eliminate **pretend** listening and **selective** listening. When you don't have the time, energy, or inclination required for focused listening, a loving act would compel you to say something like this, "I don't have the energy to truly listen right now. Please let me finish this project so I can then give you my full attention."

Listening also requires empathy—the ability to set aside your own prejudices and ideas and step into the shoes of your loved one. When you actively listen with empathy, you totally accept the other person. You hear and *feel* what is being said as well as what is not being said.

The art of listening, an act of love, requires energy, focus, and skill. Here are some listening tips:

- Stop talking. You can hear a lot by being quiet.
- Watch the speaker. Pay attention to body language.
- Listen for central themes.
- Ask questions when you are unclear about what's being said.
- Reflect back: "I hear you saying such and such. Is that correct?"

34

Be A Good Parent

To Keep Your Lover, Be A Good Parent. Love, respect and trust, open communication, commitment, and consistency mark good parents and happy families. Parents must be relaxed and forgiving and, at the same time, firm and consistent. Good parents walk that thin and narrow line of parenthood, avoiding being overgratifying and overdemanding.

The foundation for being consistent parents demands good communication between husband and wife. Children can split this foundation by playing one parent against the other. To prevent children from splitting their parents requires that the parents talk to each other away from the children, come to an agreement on the rules, and not make important decisions alone.

Cultivating a good family life that gives children the confidence that they can master just about anything depends on teaching children responsibility by establishing clear rules and regulations and punishment for breaking the rules. The punishment should fit the crime (poor school grades, for example—no TV for a week; coming home late—no use of the family car for a week, etc.). By establishing rules with understanding, flexibility and love, parents have the privilege of giving their children security and stability, a sense of confidence, a sense of importance, a belief that they can face whatever they must.

35

Have A Strong Financial Base

To Keep Your Lover, Have A Strong Financial Base. Possibly more relationship friction results from money matters than any other concern. That's too bad because the rules for a solid financial base are extremely simple. Notice I wrote simple, not easy. The rules are simple—**spend less than you earn; a lifetime of consistent, steady investment produces financial wealth**—but extremely difficult to follow. Nonetheless adopt these guidelines and your financial worries will be minimal:

- Live on 80% of your income.
- Give 10% of your income to your church, synagogue or favorite charity (this rule forces you to focus on what you have been given).
- Save 10% of your income until you have enough emergency money stashed away to cover your salary base for 6-12 months.
- Once you have 6-12 months salary in savings then begin investing 10% of your income.
- Purchase an adequate amount of life insurance to protect your family's future.
- Use credit cards for convenience, never as a money source.
- Always pay off your credit card balance at the end of each month.
- Pay off loans as quickly as possible.
- Never borrow for luxury items.

36

Believe In A Higher Power

To Keep Your Lover, Believe In A Higher Power. There exists a force outside our being that nurtures, protects, guides and loves us. A loving life requires that we take time to communicate with this higher power that some of us call God. As with any communication, communicating with God means listening, really listening, being aware, through study, meditation and cultivation of those experiences that enrich the soul. Communication with God means asking in prayer for those virtues that make life worthwhile: love, joy, peace of mind, wisdom, humility, kindness and gentleness, courage, self-control, patience, and faith.

Daily prayer and meditation improves our awareness and love for God. We love God by appreciating all we have been given, by being grateful for opportunities and challenges. We love God by having faith in the power of good. We love God by giving our best to help others enjoy life. We love God by loving ourselves, by cultivating the abundant life, by choosing happiness and joy. We love God by believing that there is a divine plan for us that leads us to our highest good. Being aware of God enriches our lives enabling us better to love.

37

Relax

To Keep Your Lover, Relax. Relaxing enhances loving. If you rest before you get tired, you save energy for love and enjoyment.

One time-tested method for relaxing is transcendental meditation, also called the healing silence or the relaxation response. To practice this technique seek a comfortable environment away from interruptions, noise and telephones. Close your eyes and relax your muscles by repeating, "breathe in relaxation, breathe out tension." Repeat this phrase or another relaxing phrase over and over for about twenty minutes. If an intrusive thought enters your mind return to your phrase. Continue this exercise for about 20 minutes. Then open your eyes, stretch and return to normal activities. The key to relaxing is to try not to try. Just relax and let go.

38

Use I-Messages

To Keep Your Lover, Use I-Messages. If you want something, ask for it in this way: state the emotion you feel and then tell what you'd like. Here is an example of how to use the I-message: "I love being with you. Will you spend 15 minutes each day with me alone?" Here's another example: "That activity makes me angry. I would like for you to stop doing that."

Using I-messages is not self-centered. Indeed the use of I-messages helps other people know exactly where you stand. Your loved one wants to please you and when your loved one knows exactly what you want, he/she can please you better.

Unfortunately many people have the idea that direct requests are selfish. They are not. Other people have the feeling, "If he/she loved me, they would know what I want." Lovers are not mind readers. You must tell them what you want.

Loving people are likeable people because they are open, honest and direct. You always know where you stand with them.

Loving people also take into account the rights and feelings of others and because they communicate openly, conflicts are easier to resolve. Let me repeat: Loving people always take into account the rights and feelings of others. That means that while openness is important you must be kind and understanding when you directly express your feelings.

39

Think Positively

To Keep Your Lover, Focus On The Positive. Lovers concentrate on the 80% that is right in their lives rather than the 20% that is wrong. And old English church inscription reminds visitors: "Think and Thank." Lovers stress the positive. They realize that attitude is more important than facts. They also realize that we become what we think about.

If you think positively you'll become a positive person. If you think negatively you'll become bitter and resentful. If you think happy thoughts you'll be happy. Or as the Roman Emperor Marcus Aurelius said, "Our life is what our thoughts make it."

Be alert to negative words and thoughts and replace them immediately with something positive. To be a good lover take these five words out of your vocabulary: *should, ought, must, always* and *never.* Stop analyzing, ruminating, criticizing and locking yourself into negative thought patterns. Stop blaming.

Count your abundance not your shortages. Praise more. Talk like a happy person. Pretend if you have to. Positive words and thoughts, even if you fake them, have the power to set in motion complex biological changes which will make you feel better.

40

Love Yourself

To Keep Your Lover, Love Yourself. Self-love is not standing in front of the mirror and saying, "You are beautiful; I love you so." That's called narcissism and some psychiatrists will lock you up for that. Self-love is not thinking of ourselves to the exclusion of others. It is not the pursuit of wealth, power and beauty. Self-love is a healthy development of our talents and a humble acceptance of our limitations.

If you love yourself you work on improving your personality and character—you allow your feelings to shine through in spontaneity and good will; you laugh freely and see the joy in daily experiences; you recognize the need for affection and tenderness; and you bring delight into relationships. If you love yourself you grow to become more spiritually aware, to realize that there is a power in the universe that is the source of all love and peace.

41

Pay Attention To Daily Disciplines

To Keep Your Lover, Pay Attention To Daily Disciplines. Discipline yourself to pay attention to the good and, as much as possible, ignore the bad. Discipline will enhance your relationship. Discipline means watching the predilection to drift, the tendency to drudge through our individual routines while ignoring the wants and needs of the other. Drifting can best be avoided by making certain that we allow time to be alone with each other: a daily stroll, an extra cup of coffee in the morning, a weekend away once a month, a dinner out at least once a week. These small daily disciplines can help us appreciate each other, help avoid the feeling of being married to a stranger.

42

Live Each Day Fully

To Keep Your Lover, Determine That You Will Enjoy Each Day To The Fullest. Lovers live fully by determining that for each day they will be happy. Each day they adjust themselves to what is and do not try to change anyone or anything. Each day they take care of their bodies. Each day they improve their minds by learning something useful. Each day they do a good deed for someone. Each day they work on being agreeable, courteous and liberal with praise. Each day they write down their goals and plans. Each day they eliminate hurry and indecision. Each day they have a quiet half hour to relax and think of God. Each day they are unafraid to enjoy what is beautiful. Each day they love and believe that those they love, love them.

43

Control Anger

To Keep Your Lover, Learn To Control Your Anger. Anger is hard on the body and the spirit. If you hold it in, it tightens you up and closes you down. On the other hand, if you let out your anger you may hurt yourself in other ways—lashing out at someone you care about, saying something you will later regret.

When angry, try to walk away from the confrontation. Avoid physical hitting, name calling, bringing up the past, sarcasm, ridicule, yelling, sulking, blaming, analyzing the other person, the silent treatment, not looking at the other person, threats or any actions that assault the worth of the other person. These insults are the great destroyers of any relationship.

To control anger try to understand it. Maybe your anger stems from selfishness, the expectation of perfection or fear of rejection. If so, walk away. Cool down.

On the other hand, sometimes anger is appropriate. Has your lover hurt you? Has your lover hurt himself/herself? If so, then express your anger: "I am upset by your behavior. I want you to stop that now!"

The best antidote for anger is empathy—the ability to put yourself in your lover's shoes and understand how he/she is feeling. When you can do that successfully, you can almost always diffuse your own anger.

44

Forget The Past

To Keep Your Lover, Forget The Past. Lovers do not allow past events to interfere with their joy and their love. They learn from their mistakes and change maladaptive behavior patterns.

Lovers realize that guilt is a needless emotion, a pseudo-punishment which allows us to continue to do those things that we feel guilty about. The best way to deal with guilt is to ask for forgiveness, to forgive yourself, to quit doing what you are doing and resolve to do better.

Likewise, regret is a tremendous waste of energy. There are some who waste hours playing "what if" or "if only" games. When you find yourself regretting remember Lot's wife—she looked back and turned into a pillar of salt. Perhaps these time-tested aphorisms will help: "You can't saw sawdust;" "Don't cry over spilt milk." Remember no one is perfect. We all make mistakes. Lovers learn from their mistakes but they refuse to regret their mistakes.

Lovers accept responsibility for their own behavior. They don't blame the past, their mothers, their fathers, their teachers, their wives, their husbands or their God for their problems. Or as Satchel Paige, who is arguably the best pitcher ever to throw a baseball said, "Don't look back, something might be gaining on you!"

45

Enjoy The Ordinary

To Keep Your Lover, Find Enjoyment In The Ordinary. Laugh at yourself and those things you can't change and strive to be creatively alive by cultivating a playful, childlike spirit.

Harold Kushner, author of *When All You've Ever Wanted Isn't Enough*, says that he believes "The happiest people work on being kind, helpful and reliable and happiness sneaks into their lives." Lovers realize that life is a series of moments and living each moment with joy, enhances love.

46

Accept Change

To Keep Your Lover, Accept Change As An Orderly Part Of The Universe. Realize that change is invigorating and stimulating. Understand that life is too short to be miserable. When you find yourself being miserable that's a sign that it's time to make changes. If you don't like your job start looking for something that will stimulate you to grow. Learn a new skill. Read something that inspires or excites you. Be open to different approaches and receptive to new ideas. Remember change is a way of growing and when you grow you become a better lover. Taking the risk to change is a loving act.

The process of growing toward independence is the process of risk taking. The more risks we take the more independent we become and consequently the more loving we can be. There is tremendous risk throughout our lives: the first day at school, the first day at camp, the first date, the first car, the first day at college, the first job, the first move away from home. With each risk we take, however, we become more confident, more worldly. The more confident and the more autonomous we are the more we can love with no strings attached. The more you risk change by doing something different, the more you grow and the more you can contribute to the growth of your lover.

47

Give Compliments

To Keep Your Lover, Know When And How To Give Compliments. Randolph K. Sanders, Ph.D., in his book, *Speak Up*, says "Giving people compliments is one of the most important communication skills in life." Compliments motivate and bring people closer together. Good compliments are specific. For example, instead of telling your lover, "You're a great person," be more specific by saying something such as, "I really like the way you show you care for me by cleaning the table and taking out the trash every day. Your attention to little details like that makes me feel appreciated and loved. Thank you." Compliment more. Compliment specifically. Compliment enthusiastically.

48

Stay In Shape

To Keep Your Lover, Stay In Shape. Lovers take care of their bodies through proper conditioning, moderate diet and healthy habits. You don't have to have a perfect body. You don't need to be a "10." Just take care of yourself.

Research has shown that those who exercise regularly, but moderately, and eat properly can increase a healthy life span by almost two decades. Thirty minutes of brisk walking, three times weekly, is enough exercise to keep your heart and lungs healthy. The key to exercise is consistency—keeping after it year after year. Moderation in dieting is appropriate, too. Avoid extremes. Being too thin is just as harmful to a relationship as being overweight. Eat enough to give you energy. Don't overeat. Avoid snacks. Avoid excessive sugar. Also, of course, if you drink alcoholic beverages, drink moderately.

To love your lover appropriately, requires a good self-image. Loving also requires energy and vitality. Take care of yourself and you'll be a better lover.

49

Do Your Best

To Keep Your Lover, Do Your Best. Trying to be perfect can disgust your loved one. Doing your best is enough. At the end of each day ask yourself this question: "Did I do my best?" If you can answer yes, you'll remove a lot of causes for negative thoughts. Now don't get this mixed up with, "Did I do everything right?" We all know that no one does everything right. Don't defeat yourself by trying the impossible. Just do your best—that's all anyone can do.

All of us are inferior in one way or another. We can always find someone who is smarter, richer, prettier, or funnier than we are. Be satisfied with the best you can be and avoid comparing yourself to others.

As football coach Lou Holtz has indicated, the rules for good living are : 1) do the best you can; 2) do what's right; and 3) follow the Golden Rule—treat others as you would like to be treated. Following those three rules will build your self-esteem and keep you from worrying about who's smarter, richer, prettier or funnier than you are. After all, those things just don't matter if you do the best you can.

50

Adopt A Holistic Lifestyle

To Keep Your Lover, Be Vibrantly Alive By Cultivating A Holistic Lifestyle. A holistic lifestyle is one of balanced moderation devoted to spiritual growth, emotional well-being and physical health. Holistically healthy people have well-toned muscles and a supple but erect posture. When they walk into a room, the room begins to vibrate with energy and enthusiasm, yet they have an inner contentment, marked by humility and self acceptance that attracts others to them. They live fully in the present, radiating sunshine almost always. They can laugh at themselves and take responsibility for their mistakes. They don't allow setbacks to discourage them. They are always striving to improve but they accept themselves where they are now. They are generous with praise and value others as much as they value themselves. They have a deep, abiding faith in God. They laugh freely, love deeply and hope always.

Biographical Sketch

John Ingram Walker, M.D. and his wife Vicki have been married for 26 years. They have two children, Wende and Brad. Dr. Walker lectures on emotional growth. Vicki coordinates his speeches, listens to them and gives constructive comments.

Yes, I would like additional copies of 50 Ways To Keep Your Lover.

Please send me________copies at $9.95 per copy $___________
Sales Tax (Texas residents only) $ .77/copy ___________
Add $2.50 for postage and handling ___________

Name:______________________________
Address:______________________________
City:__________________ State:______________ Zip______________

Credit Card #______________________ Exp. Date______________
Type (MasterCard/Visa, etc.)______________________________

Also available by telephone or mail order:

	Book Cost		Sales Tax*		Postage & Handling	
A Life Well Lived	$15.95	+	$1.24	+	$2.50	________
Everybody's Guide To Emotional Well-Being	$ 9.95	+	$ .77	+	$2.50	________
Best Of The Self Help Books	$ 7.95	+	$ .62	+	$2.50	________
Jim Reid's Winning Basketball	$ 8.95	+	$ .70	+	$2.50	________
Total Self-Help - *6 Tape Series*	$59.95	+	$4.65	+	$2.50	________

TOTAL ORDER $________

*(Sales Tax for Texas residents only)

Walker Communications
876 Loop 337 Bldg. D, Suite #401
New Braunfels, Texas 78130
(512) 629-7303

Yes, I would like additional copies of 50 Ways To Keep Your Lover.

Please send me ________ copies at $9.95 per copy	$__________
Sales Tax (Texas residents only) $ .77/copy	__________
Add $2.50 for postage and handling	__________

Name: ______________________________

Address: ______________________________

City: ______________ State: ______________ Zip ______________

Credit Card # ______________________ Exp. Date ______________

Type (MasterCard/Visa, etc.) ______________________________

Also available by telephone or mail order:

	Book Cost		Sales Tax*		Postage & Handling	
A Life Well Lived	$15.95	+	$1.24	+	$2.50	________
Everybody's Guide To Emotional Well-Being	$ 9.95	+	$ .77	+	$2.50	________
Best Of The Self Help Books	$ 7.95	+	$ .62	+	$2.50	________
Jim Reid's Winning Basketball	$ 8.95	+	$ .70	+	$2.50	________
Total Self-Help - *6 Tape Series*	$59.95	+	$4.65	+	$2.50	________
	TOTAL ORDER					$________

*(Sales Tax for Texas residents only)

Walker Communications

876 Loop 337 Bldg. D, Suite #401

New Braunfels, Texas 78130

(512) 629-7303

Yes, I would like additional copies of 50 Ways To Keep Your Lover.

Please send me________copies at $9.95 per copy $___________
Sales Tax (Texas residents only) $ .77/copy ___________
Add $2.50 for postage and handling ___________

Name:____
Address:____
City:____________________ State:_______________Zip______________

Credit Card #_________________________ Exp. Date________________
Type (MasterCard/Visa, etc.)_________________________________

Also available by telephone or mail order:

	Book Cost		Sales Tax*		Postage & Handling	
A Life Well Lived	$15.95	+	$1.24	+	$2.50	________
Everybody's Guide To Emotional Well-Being	$ 9.95	+	$ .77	+	$2.50	________
Best Of The Self Help Books	$ 7.95	+	$ .62	+	$2.50	________
Jim Reid's Winning Basketball	$ 8.95	+	$ .70	+	$2.50	________
Total Self-Help - *6 Tape Series*	$59.95	+	$4.65	+	$2.50	________

TOTAL ORDER $________

*(Sales Tax for Texas residents only)

Walker Communications
876 Loop 337 Bldg. D, Suite #401
New Braunfels, Texas 78130
(512) 629-7303